Emblems of Earth and Light

Emblems of Earth and Light

Poems by

R.J. Hejna

Cover design by Shay Culligan
Cover image by Yuheng Ouyang on Unsplash
Author photo by Heidi McClelland

ISBN: 979-8-90146-817-3
Library of Congress Control Number: 2026934960

Kelsay Books
502 South 1040 East, A-119
American Fork, Utah 84003
Kelsaybooks.com

Acknowledgments

Thank you to the following publications, in which versions of these poems previously appeared:

Encore: "Center-Seed"

Hopwood Award: "Jupiter Explored," "Wooden Madonna," "Enigma"

Penwood Review: "Nocturne" (revised, retitled "Song for a Newborn Daughter")

Sow's Ear Review: "Grandpa Frankie's Notes"

A most heartfelt thank you to my dear friend and fellow poet, Ken Meisel, for his profound encouragement and support.

Also, thank you to my dear brother and fellow poet, Jim Hejna for shared critiques over the years, and laughs over such topics as "syntax".

And thank you to Heidi McClelland, photographer, for her excellent portrait.

Finally, love and appreciation to my wife, Malena, for her instillment of hope.

Contents

Barn-Houses of Yore

Open-Air Museum, Black Forest, Germany

Still in this Swartzwald vale,
down the valley steps of time,
honeybees harvest pollen from
blooms of hollyhock where far
ago medieval folk bent to foster
the lineage of stalks, so fertile
that yearly sentinel of clowns
in pastel'd mirth posed there
to illumine burdened moods
of the Scheunenhausen. Yes,

those relic hulks, home to my
centuries-old kin, to their oxen,
cows, swine and sheep, were
stained dark as the rich earth
that pushed up and held wheat,
dark with few windows, dark in
not knowing why things moved
and ceased moving, therefore
stained sullen in superstition
as the dreams of their keepers.

Some dreams. Others spawned
the mills and looms, and spoke
softly by oil lamp light, coo'd
the babes, and filled the lofts
with the hope of baking bread.
Benefit was had, with no walls
between folk and four legged;
mutual warmth, sustenance

made the dark less dark, and
fostered melody from longing.

But what drama haunts a cow's
sleep, or a sow's? Grass dreams,
mud dreams, being fully sired
by a bull or boar in a hot field?
Had such fodder stowed away
in journeys to the deeper mind
of my ancestral kin, sowed
influence felt in moist teasing
of shared, somnolent breaths,
the beast lust, and folk lust?

Abandon, let go, release seed
like the hollyhock, so prolific;
yet, in abandon one may covet
a strong or tender hand fairly
vowed to another, and from
such tilted yearning will come
tilted result, as wheat sown
from rotten source must grow
stunted or bitter, lacking in
pure goodness for its reason.

So, struggle to tame what lures
a bud to burst, hence to suffer
on and on, generations of kin.
How to survive a last breath?
Blame it on the misfits, tilted
ones who soared on sad brooms
high above Geist Mountain.
Build a wooden cross, post it
with salvation hung in agony
there among the hollyhocks.

Now, as shadows reach long
across your fallow fields, tell us,
wise and solemn folk-byres:
What sense is unburied there,
what reconciled hospice for all
which is evolving on its own,
all which endeavors the more,
all which aches to understand,
reach for, grab and love, so as
not to sink under and give in?

Fading into the Field

In Memoriam for Theodore Roethke

Across the clearing, places of light
move through haze, now freed,
epiphanies perhaps
recently set loose from a tangle
of melancholic string,
or emancipated musings
no longer bound
in a mind so ragged it could
touch a word
until it bled.

This is Ted's place, where perhaps
roams his resolution, a tactic
to be perfected as fume
of a dead weed, at last sure,
shivered in poplars.
Everyone's a cutting, are they not?
And all bent on the impossible.
Gravity is defied by seasons,
so the smells, the rapture
of passing lifts us
up, like Nijinsky's
winged shoes.

Suppose Ted's last moment
could have defined it,
sent it to the fire as so:
Roots choke. Stones dig
into the final conundrum.
Last breath of the fruity dungeons
fermented in a toad, now
rally the grasshopper legions
as my plowshare furrows through!
Why live? Why not forever?
Light is chewed up. An anvil
resounds from a core.

Of All the Senses, Touch

For Emily Dickinson

Of all the senses, touch
is most immediate, exacting,
the fingers identifying
in a thing its gift or its bane.

To take some holiness
or blessing from a porcelain
likeness of the Virgin,
or cow in a Shinto shrine,

and put it to one's heart
or sore place of imbalance
surely will restore light
and bring mercy to a wrong.

But how to touch a poem,
I'd like to know, Emily, a way—
whether to ingest one
you'd penned on parchment,

slowly chewing your words
would be my way to eucharist,
shed my dull, lowly slough
and be healed of being alive?

The Capuchin Crypt

Chapel of Bones, Rome

What you are now, we used to be.
What we are now, you will be.
—The Monks

What we forget to notice, a swallow shearing through
the somber shade, a mouse twiddle from flat stone
to flat stone, is a loss we cannot afford.

Ten thousand or more bones, columns rowed, arches put
skull, to skull, to skull which are not all vacant
there, they will oversee this garden;

this garden which is not the bones, but their desire, and
not for having flesh but the honesty not to need
flesh and therefore, to be here, fully.

It was like so: a brother passed, and having ministered
to the poor that theirs was inheritance of light,
he took the thirty-year spot of another,

leading by example—that a bone, once freed had only
the pulp of its message which was, in its odd
placement, maintaining a finer grace.

Footsteps make their tentative parlay, as we harvest here,
forgetting to notice the bones have stolen laughter,
and bestowed it to the wretched.

Etude for Autumn

Ever saw a flock take flight,
their stretch and pull
like signs of plus and minus—
math has brought us here
and will take us away.

I saw you there, by the mill, by the river's stones
standing as though you'd been there
for years in your red flannel
in a photo I'd kept
on the piano.

Ever heard the count of caw,
crows telling numbers
like necromancers read
news that hasn't yet come
by light in a black place.

It was somehow September again, another smile
had seemed to dress your face as if
things would end differently,
like a dove had landed
on the pastor.

Ever turned the fallow field,
knowing when to know
like a wave’s time to curl over,
what must measure a loss
to sow the sweeter gain.

I imagined the mill wheel turning the splashes
of river behind you, bringing about
a stillness that still might
satisfy what no one
has yet explained.

Destiny Is Relative

On the passing of Albert Einstein

Quiet, patient, helpless trees,
standing in shapes of prayer,
their trunks I lean against,
and through which my
thoughts transcend to solve
what was unsolvable, as
epiphany, mass within light;
these are their enemies,
the words, emblems of will.

Old, yearning, reaching ones,
trusting in myths of season
to perhaps at last tow for us the
boulder over the high hill's rim—
surely, once winter freezes
branch by branch the flame
that borrows my intent,
I will go and rest among
the days they have buried,
with planets around my head.

The Hounds of Valor

D-day

Tireless, though eyes dragged
like Roosevelt's near the end,
they are at every valiance there
to sound their abandon note,
though especially at Overlord,
the beaches where one slogged
through the waves, carbine
held aloft, and defiantly yelled
and yelled right through heat
from the slug that slammed
into one's chest and everything
turned into another thing, parts
of angels whirled out through
a dismay of galaxies—ah, yes,
that's when the hounds arrive
in their panting slobber, put
their heads back, and give us
the abandon sound, the one to
follow far off to the before, to
the wellhead, to the first inhale.

The Preserved Couple's Embrace

Pompeii, Italy

They were not celebrated ones,
not heralded, exalted by masses

oh my whispering dear

as more than imperious, more
a part or purveyor of the divine;

never cease whispering

and hence lie here not in silk,
not with scepter or gold glyphs—

when the lark's song falters

in fact, less than stark Plebeian—
now anonymous, baked in ash.

and jasmine shrivels sour

No, what found them veneration
here, where anyone can see, is

I will stay in your arms

they hold the shape of light
in clay, ever clasping something

and all else shall pass away

for which we all must yearn, high
or mighty we may have been.

Jupiter Explored

In honor of Rainer Maria Rilke

Those of us very far in advance,
or very meek, join meanings
like vines, invisible in the
infinite hues of Jovian landscape.

There are frames for our future souls,
our frozen energies held tight
in the Ionian glaciers—dwarfed
satellites of supreme crystal.

For you, Rainer, if you could know
the latest data—how perplexing!
Even their God leaves a trail
like an essence of profound *dog-ness*.

Finally, traveling toward the Process,
itself in a structure of ellipses
and bodies of glass harmony—
our paths become forever imaginary.

Claiming the Anima

Into pillars and flame
far above the gods' mountain,
I soared to my full height,
and there among the winged
and majestic—invincible,
I won you. Not by ordinary
contest of sentiment,
desire or test of strength,
not by professed faith, or rescue,
not through any play or slight—
no, in a ray of thought
I breathed you in. Your warrior's
curves, your elegance
of blade and spear—not
what I expected, not svelte
or enticing, nor demure in grace,
but more a thunderbolt
zinged to the blood,
leaving its after-flash there
against the opulent clouds, my
oracle's release, armored
starlight—a memory, imprint
of flowering tree, my instinct
in tapered nakedness,
dropping petals that
floated, innocent,
down.

Soliloquy of the Cyclops

Thunder! Thunder! Lightning, more lightning!
I am of the Sky and the Earth!
First illuminate, and from this awaken.
My purpose! My sacred pattern! The sound
of air being cloven, clapped into thought
in motion, into a new way to see—such is
vision. One has to see from the center
to will such things, and so they are willed.
You see? Ha, ha! I am conscious of laughter!
Thunder! Lightning! I am blessed!
Of the sky is freedom; of earth, knowledge.
I am sired by the highest thought,
birthed by the most fertile womb, now!
Now, when I rattle the seams of the Everything.
I see potential! I see absolute solution.
I never devoured a human being—only
ignorance, and unwillingness to think free.
I am thunder! I am lightning! I exist, now!

On Hearing Rachmaninoff's Vespers, 1971

The ancestral tomb tones the buoyant breath.
I hear voices, low voices in caves.
Return, return the flower to its heart.
Replace the bond of youth in stone.
How comes this now? I wonder, and whisper:
  Choral hymns have echoed here before—
  invisible evening stars, revealed in znameny.

I send my own sound out into the darkness.
Can someone hear, and reach across the veil?
Return, my brothers, from the lost places,
  old man in the wind, child's face in the moon!
Return, my sisters, from the hard walls,
  dried up wells of bitter song, seasons to waste!

The angels of my people anticipate new flight.
I hear their wings, soft wings in the clouds.
Return, return the precious to its house.
Replace the keys of mirth in song.
What is meant? I wonder, and whisper:
  Choral hymns have echoed here before—
  invisible evening stars, revealed in znameny.[1]

---

[1] *Slavic for "sacred songs"*

Wooden Madonna

She reads the grain
of an emerging book—
a testament in her arms,
held tight as if clamped.

And with ignobleness,
as it is chipped away,
goes the threat of fire
and dull mortality.

From such timeless trees,
that which breaks off feeds
in a profound tithing. Here
is a gospel for them.

Suite from Camelot

I.
Arthur

It served him, at the end of this day,
of a time of timeless ending,
to consider a duty something more
than Merlin said was the turning
of a world around a pole.
He stood on the dark hill in rain,
stood to ponder what most matters,
what turns mordant around each
decision to confront a flaw.
Cycles fling their longing into what?
Merlin had lived inverted,
future life informing things long past.
Therefore, under tutelage, a king
might well bend whatever starlight
told events to cast a myth.
Or, both were lunatics, numbed
by law. He considered rain, and
falling, and whether dark was
inevitable. Merlin said it was, without
it nothing had begun or mattered—
because of hunger within it.

The betrayal becomes soon the
blessing? He shifted weight and
leaned upon his sword.
Footsteps in the mud, he thought,
molds left by choices made
are meditations once one has
found a path between
being led and followed. Then, a pile
of dead men's boots, like old
leaves tossed together,
may amount to something more
than a tenuous turning
of one face toward another.

II.
Guinevere

All along a golden song
she soared to her form,
and when she emerged
the sun must have sighed.

Pilgrims to her shrine swear
first stars wished on her,
tides chose by her choice
each mood of the moon.

Nothing she could want less
than being queen, nor
worse, the heroic surge
of a slaughterer's loins;

but the things came clearly
and would not relent,
as if someone taught them
and demanded result.

She birthed the last battle,
foresaw its flaming trees.
All of what grows now in
that plain is her reckoning.

III.
Lancelot

It was his duty to be born,
to serve not just majesty,
nor even divinity or its law.
What was true in a moment

would turn his head, adjust
his lance toward a need.
No hesitation as Arjuna's
begged this one for counsel.

That was all of his power,
to not think, not feel, not pray.
It was what urged him on,
as if tethered to the stone.

To make love and war were
the same for him; he rode
toward the final battle with no
concern for moon or sun—

no, with such might that by
his will night and day each
would take charge of the other.
Too late, fair Lancelot. Too late.

IV.
Camlann

Morning mist had lifted from the hills.
One stood amongst one's brothers there
to wait for a sign, an arrow to slam
into the ground at one's feet, for a charge,
to clamber down through the aster,
foxglove, and grasses, to defy with one's
last voice a thrust through the ribs.
And, as they all lay still, it was like a curtain
fell with a roar heard for many leagues,
if not out to the edges of what was known,
like a veil fallen between what was possible
and that which was foretold—an errand
run to the myth. So, a blade was hurled
to the still lake, held sudden in a hand
to insure leaves again would turn gold
around the trees like manes, and young,
impudent buds burst in following springs.
Sadness, blessed sadness reigned, and
growing things to the golden were resolved.

Notes of a Fisherman

Often in my sleep I feel under me
the hull float by itself off
toward nothing, nowhere—no horizon,
no fish, no damned sea.
I've woken pacing,
counting cracks in the floor,
and told myself, "Trust in movement!"
True, a depth cannot be tamed,
but there's a sense of riding, of balance—
fear with effort, matter leveled
as motion sends.
Matter and the land . . . at times
I've thought of lions—dusty, heavy,
they brood and breed destruction.
Like my father's fathers,
men who rode horses, trained them
for those who pillaged Rome,
I know that sense of riding—
I chose a mare.
But lions are depth to the land,
bound by laws of paradox.
I presume they dream, but not of boats
or fish nets dragged to catch
old age. As for myself,
in sleep I depend; awake
I'm burdened. The time, the tides—
erect a lighthouse—I'm drawn
toward bone. My father's fathers begot
whole towns, and became grass.

Enigma

The long barns
On the hill's horizon
The holy white horse
Whose face is lit
By the boy's blue moon
The silver water song
And guardian wave
Of Avalon
Reflected in a picture
You were escaping

The Farther Urging

References the Oscoda fire of 1911

In a hall closet there are old boots,
the black, high-top kind with laces she
and her kind would wear to school, or
to stroll along the river boardwalk
where reflections of her frill dresses
would waver because of black barges
bearing the corpses of newly cut trees.
Or to travel, mostly by steam train.

Lately, not that it was autumn, which
did always recall her ache for those trees;
not that she'd been widowed suddenly
like a dove shot out of the sky last year
on Christmas day; no, more she was led
by another, farther urging for return,
for burying nuts in a place she'd known,
she wakes and goes to the hall closet.

It's long about an owl's winking time,
when moonlight lilts in each elf-step, she
rises, puts wire-rims onto her nose, and
from a spindly bed post takes with bony
hand her mink-collared overcoat, then
pulls it over her gown, saying, "I wish
they'd have let me know." It's not dream,
but pieces, shreds of it left like wraiths.

In the hall closet she stoops, frets and
rummages, pulls and pushes at musty
stuff, umbrellas, boxes of keepsake and
letters, church hats with brooches, and
a cage, gilded, with a swing for a bird.
She sighs. A pair of boots is missing.
"Perhaps the tenants will know," she
thinks, and takes the cage to the hall.

She knocks. "Can we help?" they ask.
Dream-shreds float around her face
as it peers in, a perplexity of wrinkle.
One bony finger raised to her cheek,
she says, "Excuse me, do you know
the way to the train?" As if there was
a train horn then, "No," they reply,
"did you know you're holding a cage?"

"But it's time I was getting home,"
she persists, "they're expecting me."
Alone to a closed door, then it runs,
the tale she tells there in the hall,
of the night the whole town burned
and she was just five. It was someone
had somehow lit the mill and yards
of sad lumber stacked by the river.

So the flames reflected fury in the
wavering black water, and everyone
grabbed what they could. Her bird
was all she'd thought to grab, in its
cage, not singing. "Get to the station,"
a man yelled in the street, "go now,
get to the next town!" She'd run, one
hand in mother's, one with the cage;

but feared for the bird, whose song
was refuge in a lonesome house, like
one star in fog upon which to wish.
How dense the smoke seemed, how
hard to breathe. Such noise of voices
shouting, the poor thing. Pausing to
tend it, she'd let go the safer hand,
and in that moment become missing.

"Excuse me, do you know the way
to the train?" she'd ask of anyone.
In her telling, someone did. At least
Christmas was salvaged, and the bird.
Years had flashed through her like
mirrors in the glass of passing trains.
She'd had other birds, taught school,
and found this house with the closet.

From each year, a day had gone missing.
From each event, a task. From each telling,
a word. From each sigh, a need. Until
one night she'd begun this way of waking,
searching for the missing things, asking,
recounting with the cage held until she'd
put it on the floor, and start to fold
and unfold her hands one over the other.

It's the folding of the tale, the unfolding
of what couldn't be helped. It's about
what goes into a flame, and goes out with
less reason. So, she folds and unfolds
her hands in the dark, as if she might find
there another sort of bird, a white one;
and had she done so, might finish the tale,
raise both hands high, and set it free.

The Pharaoh

In my hallowed room
I am suspended, not
as promised, done.
These revered tools,
my scepter, my ankh
are not, it seems,
of use to transcend.
In the triangular dark,
my awareness stays,
my deeds leaned
obliquely around me.
Only the Sphinx
knows my solitude,
and it, vowed silent
in the dry wind,
has left unsolvable—
that I am the lives
of the slaves.
Surely some meaning
breathes itself into
efforts of my lot,
were I hence only
to haul stone or
be beholden to it?
Had I but seen an ibis
take flight, and
thought to free all,
I might not be here
immanent, almost—

almost more than held
in my own embrace,
wrapped in mystery
like food for a spider.

Variations on a Theme of Yeats

THE GYRES! the gyres! Old Rocky Face, look forth;
Things thought too long can no longer be thought,
For beauty dies of beauty, worth of worth,
And ancient lineaments are blotted out.
—William Butler Yeats

The gyres, indeed! The dervish whirls one hand above,
One hand below and never faints or falls, to defy
Old Carved Face, for beauty begets honesty,
And worth begets respect, never to be ignored.

Gently, the gyres! Gently look into the void, Old Face;
What goes out must ever go in again, and out,
For answers must answer to themselves,
And in such reverence the lineaments are pure.

Sing the gyres, dance the gyres! Myth of oldness;
Losses cannot outlast the letting go of loss,
For death gives life, and life gives change,
And eventually strands take root in the cure.

Embrace! Become one with ancientness, wake up;
Fortune will drag us by the napes of our necks,
For hope is in the gyres, and turns them 'round,
And lineaments weave the veils of the adored.

Oedipal Cow Poem

Madison, Wisconsin

Why will cows refuse to fall
when fired on by the best boy marksmen?
Why are sticks not rifle enough,
and fathers staid foreign to the cause?
Hand in hand, a father and son shall walk
by sides among the cows and colored leaves,
though neither speak, the ground shall
mediate what seems so grand
and seems so small.
What dies to live in a tree?
What branch, when forced to bend
knows not forgiveness?

Lie down for me, cow. Let leaves refuse to fall.
Lie down for me, cow. Be not what you are.
Be not heroic, to stand against all odds.
Lie down for me, cow. Let night
burn its way into the fields
of anonymity.

All odds be other things,
last breath rattled at a crossroads—
knowing shall become un-forbidden.
Why will cows refuse to fall, and fathers last
only until before they are finally missed?
Hand in hand, a step of the father
dies into the son's among the cows and
colored leaves to measure what stays young.
Who dares turn out dreams from a paddock?
Who would forfeit a life to grow horns?

Then aim, well as he might, the son
shall shoot, as the cow still
impudently chews; wild
voice of a stick sent into black space,
unexpected, exploding a star.

Nocturne

Elf'd in a father's arms, and sung
his measured steps to bed she is,
in the dark, swaying dark, a song—fair,
light-spun one from a mystic place
where metaphor has never reached
nor gravity tugged at a heart.

Not hymn or carol, more she lives
in a lullaby of bells, a madrigal
of streams and birds all telling news—
changes, goings, comings, how it is
for crocus and peepers in late spring
when even a choice is innocent.

How many nights might sorely fall
into the dawn she's lately become?
Never mind, love within a love,
new moon the old moon keeps.
His breath seems done by other lungs,
now, is it him or her who sleeps?

Serenade for the Wind

Sing to a surly gust! Swept ’round in a bleak place
of rock and shrill leer of hawk; this rowdy,
rude buffet unseen, sent from a sudden fold
of a sun’s ray to flex its dumb arabesque—

ah, this ancestral thing, the breeze! Generations
may turn and turn to seed and be sown, sent
in currents, stolen, flown to where the air might find
in whispered whim the perfect resting place.

From whence came the first rouse, like the first
yawn of knowing which had been curled
in some leafy corner, then sucked in surprise
to tumult out all the planets and stars?

It cannot be, now is the instant I will become
and go in and out and around to flex by
every open line; though I may choose to sing
on the wings of my high, haunted desire.

And so, it takes a blow to make a song, a breath
through narrow space, a slivered line betwixt
the way things should and shouldn’t be, although
ever refreshed and new, note kaleidoscope’d.

Mona Lisa Sonata

On Viewing the Original Painting

I.

I spend my moments in thought of movement.
In a rose and stone is the essence of desire—change.
A rose that blooms, a stone that stays—verily, such
mysteries have their tempo. Perchance, I am
the world on a wall, as it dreams itself fine
moments of resolution. I should say, there need
be no other life—my gaze, as much the riddle;
and in it, there I turn to and fro darkly, as a cloak
revolves in wind. Time ferments my rumor; thus,
I am an hourglass loaned to a host of dying clowns,
and remain steadfast in my disputed role
as the mirror of eternal smiles.

II.

I shall never lose the subtleness of age as
it is not mine. I am aware, imminent
in delivery, a furthering of what could be,
oiled alive, ardor in a dust of moments.
My source is serpentine, fever in a lake,
yet if fecundity is sought, seek elsewhere.
Invention's my delight—ah, to breathe design!
Surely, as fruit must fall without my knowing,
beauty numbs the eye of my absence.
A thing is ripe to know itself when it knows
it's everlasting. So, my furtive mirth endures
beyond the thought of distant mountains.

III.

I have a sign from ancient myth
that lights my vision more than any sun.
I have reversed life into itself with an arrangement
of my hands, and reflect a dreamer's way
of moving. Grant a wish and go, grant it to yourself,
the impetus. Return time to its owner, it is a mask
on the face of serenity. Everyone is posed
in the moment they are more than they imagined.
Compare a rose to stone, and know everlasting
in a mood. Beyond my cloak, a waterfall of change—
I, in my disputed role remain steadfast,
as the mirror of eternal smiles.

Tending to Respite

Black Forest, Germany

Where is no need for mowing,
where a cherished clunk of
neck-bells un-tolls time for all
the few still living, off a ridge
of soldier'd spruce in Swartzvald—
there could be the village plot
of memory stones, among which
moos and ripping tufts prevail;
tending done by those who rest,
more subtle, more silent, faint
sense or fume of sudden resolve
one gets, and so it's a fair trade
for heifer to tend there the grass.

Where near is the kneeling place,
where one thousand Candlemas
had shone down a grander flame
to all the few; shelter, sustenance
there, too, for a winter'd udder—
there could be a sacred tale told,
how one of those eves a pregnant,
horned-one hoofed to chancel,
stood and lowed till ushered out.
So, the alliance was made for all
to be pastoral, tend to respite,
to co-mingle, sins half-absolved
by the blessed lows and bells.

Loons Opening a Blind Man's Eyes

Inspired by Inuit artist, Davidialuk

The two loons
converse inside
an illuminated
circle, facing one
another and
suspended, beak-
speaking
among shades
of iridescence.
One loon pretends
to fall asleep,
luring us to see
without seeing.
The other
lifts on one foot
in ritual, conjuring
memory of sight.
They say loons
can see deep
in dark water—
that is worth
more than pearls.
The one who would
be healed has
strange anesthetic.
Is he sure there
are loons? It is hard
to know this, because

the feet of him rise
up from the bottom
into the healing
circle, his head still
upside down
somewhere only
he can see.
Perhaps the loons
are opening his eyes.
Perhaps he is learning
how to walk in
the middle of the air.

Pythagoras

No one cares what Pythagoras[2] in his prime
did, meandering down the bank of a river
in search of a right-angled hunk of stone, and
stopping to eat oat mush from an old clay jar.

It might have been evening or dawn, and the
same bright orb could have told its legend there
in the same sky some Pythagorean, robust
woman who may or may not have borne him

babes might or might not have noticed, and been
another honesty. No one documented things
like that. By him, a mind was thought to bend
in sequence, like a willow would in melody

play the lyre of resolution—light and dark, which
gives us our purpose. Simple, mathematical
kindness. Such a stubborn, irrational number
was the mystical, square-root of his sides.

---

[2] *There are conflicting stories—some say he married, others say he was single. They agree he wouldn't eat beans, and played the lyre. He allegedly refused to run through a bean field to escape his murderer.*

None Are Enemies

Reinfeld, Germany

Also the enemy mourns its fallen ones,
its heroes more or less—those
who'd followed a call like geese and seasons,
but to untimely ends.
None still are enemies that lie down
to fill the sore earth.
In Reinfeld, an unimposing wall of stone,
curved where people stroll or play,
holds the plaques of brass, each with name of one
the allied forces got, evidently
one aligned with the wrong view.
None still are enemies that stood
to test the lasting doubt.
Atoms to atoms, bleakness in the end
becomes daffodil. There were
mothers here whose sacrifice
of what matters rails in the womb.
None still are enemies that fill
the night sky with stars.
And so, irony frayed in the wind mends, while
damp winters passing still try to stain
the old plaques more green.
None are enemies.
None are enemies.

Grandpa Frankie's Notes

Descended from gypsies, he used to say,
so the violin came more honest than words.
Though an absurdity, still, like a deaf crow
on a rough street he stole the notes that
wafted, flew off lines of laundry dangled out
between tenement windows, pinned there
after a fight with a dear drunken imbecile,
notes that tumbled off belfries on the wings
of pigeons slanting this way and that when
the bells woke them and the drunks below,
notes that journeyed across the murderous
sea, those that previously wove the thatch
of village huts and stoked their sullen fires,
turned the wheels of mud-wagon'd lanes
and urged the days from the gut of a town crier,
in that Czech vlast where the whole land
reverberated like inside the piano above
where he sat hidden under a blanket, his
sister playing Dvorak he was forbidden;
so he got those notes in his travels, black-
wing solos, took them out once he'd found
the violin, pulling them out like hocked
necklaces from a coat sleeve to serenade
here or there a bent-over couple for a coin.
Then they belonged also to the violin he
kept by his pillow like a lover, his arm draped
over at night, so he could feel its delicate
curves, notes of vagabond sing to his sleep,
sing the miraculous grace of Vltava River,
its moorings where notes were sent, received,

passed along with word, news, stories from
up-river, down-river all this the river, like
blood sent along to mend huge loneliness.
At his funeral, I placed a crow wing-feather
in the button hole over his heart. As they
lowered the casket, a crow flew in from the
east, circled over twice, and off to the west.
It took all those stolen notes, the shiny ones
someone left on a table, the odd plaintive
ones someone sent to the clouds from a
plank porch, the magnificent ones orated
in prayer, in poems, in what is between
two sets of eyes looking a very long time,
took them to the land of souls, where
those winged, waiting with the bowed heads
were in some unfathomable way nourished.

Stalemated in a Stare

It's your craft, inconstant flame
that holds this long-kept thing
in check. I am rook to my emotion,
tamed, stalemated in a stare.
My stomach turns knights' strategies.
My head rides the bishops' sidelong path.
Ah, I've moth'd myself in levels
toward the light, and learned no more
of this long-kept thing, than that it
holds me here. I cannot move away
my king. Every bit of subject left
in his castle loves its enemy.
So fly me a golden arrow, or heart-
shaped stone of siege! If it's to count,
the score must move by trust integral.
Otherwise end it swift crossways,
and I shall rise straight from ash.

Elizabethan Date

In a room of white stone
and marble curving stair,
stringed instruments move
the air ancient, delicate.
As many seated pose
in proper attire, she may
shine in rays of sun, silent
as statue, pedestaled.

But could one stir in her
a small flame, by music
tweaked to strum, she may
find plumes and masks
on us all, faces powdered
too fine, too bold, fanning
jealousy off, fanning off
deceit of sly affairs.

Then, as bass notes plough
in steady hoof steps
her fields, she may find
herself amongst peasant
folk, plank tables at inns,
with bards droning on
for bawdy suitors drunken
brawls, and sassy bottoms
ruff and velveteen.

Up From the Horizon

Inspired by Inuit artists, Kenojvak/Lukta

The long-winged loons
fly back and forth, fill everything
in a herringbone design.
Up from the horizon, feathers on diagonal,
flying to and fro
with their rudder tails.
They make a fabric of dream,
upon which one might depend
for longevity.
Because of the harmony of loons,
the humor of loons, one may sing and laugh
to a further winter.
A child on the tundra
holds up its arms wide to embrace their gifts.
They have given it a dream.
Their wings are enormous, filling everything
up from the horizon, making a link of loon
ancestor to Inuit ancestor
in this trusting one who dreams long loon-journeys
to the Atlantic,
their finding of mates, and return.
It's because of his dream, they find their way.
Little bundled figure reaching up,
up from the horizon.
On either side, a dog
is startled, barking for the spirit child, barking
at the improbability of flight,
barking about things
only dogs can know.

Into the Slow River

In a land swelling abundance,
we host a blood-let of honor,
our cry for pity allowed to poach
where roams our measure.
 Sorrow, many mistake for empty,
 while to own is, with envy twinned,
 orphaned in wrath, as even law
 twists to every advantage.
What is it we see there? Does
a mountain reflect on extremes?
It's time to be more than fodder.
More than survive, we must meld
together, blend brooks, streams
of self, our residue sifted, our
silt and peat of heritage tumbled
through forest, rock, tilled fields,
and on toward transformation.
What do we hear in denial
of need? Does a breeze live on
resistance? More is in the asking.
More is an abundant thought.
Winning is just. As losing is just.
We have all we ever deserve.

So let us dance an evolving dance
and turn up at a bountiful place,
where insight takes hunger
and ignites it, where wisdom
takes sorrow and ferments it,
where honor takes abundance
and balances it, as a mother
would bathe but redeem us,
future leaders of the free,
with a nudge into the slow river.

Coral at Cozumel

Angel and parrot fish
in colors portray the divine
respectively, devout or
festival, little mimes of
what is found inland.

A ruin perhaps, sanctuary
at one time, tumbled
stone and half old arch,
now surrounded by farm,
one might discover.

An elder might pass,
face furrowed in midday
heat, disregarding chickens
clucking where once
there was an altar.

On a nearby porch,
Senorita dances to prepare
for her role today, bright
skirt flying, hand claps
echoed by ancestors.

One may pray and live;
one may laugh and succumb.
Clowns are another
sort of angel.
An altar is in our view.

Paramour

Then with farewell in whisper,
and only then he'll pull anchor,
flags flourished as for the kings of old,
and rove away to the tropics.

Sure as on high seas, he may
slipper a foot with fair wind,
let the deck-man's song fill a calve's sail full,
and teeth undo the ropes

for a drift in the scintillant moon
toward sand, toward drums, and fire.
There he'll host the olive skin dance, oiled,
sweaty, limber, belly to belly.

Constellations

My old friends, pinned
into the cloak of night like
broaches, insignia of insight, just
as well snuffed as stayed,
they are the designs of
what could have been.
Still where, still there, after all
efforts have trembled, wept
into the broken mirrors,
ridden through a narrow hole;
I might've been the one
with the club, or shepherd's gift
for seeing what's gone.
Star light, star bright, I conjured
one of their sons to fall at my
command, in the moment,
in the line—what was lost?
I could refuse knowledge, even
my authority, but not them.
No, their possibility is relentless.
Could I last, as ambassador?

Center-Seed

Accompaniment for Dance

You move from a core—
center-seed, luminous, un-manifest,
known while you were young,
but long left dormant.
You look back in, gather, filter, sift—
discover that the segments form a line,
and the line bends
by rules you've always known.
Evolve, emerge,
hoist up from the mud, body-moves,
leaps, and turns.
Arms fit with horizons. Hips and thighs
hold their own realm.
Ribs remember moon,
pearl. Interiors open.
Go as rings roll from where a stone enters in.
Increase, push out, and purify. Feel fresh.
Marsh bog. Tadpoles. Yellow lilies.

Woman Transformed into a Sea

Inspired by Inuit artist, Davidialuk

The loon's beak turns to the left.
Half wing, the hand;
half web, the foot.
One moment ago she'd been Inuit,
alone. Her husband drowned
while hunting seals
a whole season before.
She'd been sitting, unable to eat,
thinking of her husband,
his new home, no one to care.
Now, she is immutably half loon,
but she is losing her shape.
The loons are doing it
with their lonesome shaman's calls.
Winter sky and sea are one.
Half wing, the hand.
Half web, the foot.
Not disconsolate, she looks one way,
then the other, ready
for loon calls, and the unknowable.
Then, she is half substance,
startled by her own cry. Ai!
The arctic sea bird descends—blue! Blue!
Suddenly a crack in the ice—
loon-woman falling through.
Water fills her wing fingers,
and web toes, her last loon call making
an echo of waves
becoming frozen.

About the Author

R.J. Hejna is of French, German, and Czechoslovakian descent. He holds a master's degree from University of Michigan, where he received a Hopwood Award for a book of poetry in 1979. From 1979 to 1982, he read his work as part of performances by a collective of dancers, pianist, and photographer called *Solo Alliance.* His poems have appeared in periodicals such as *Bardic Echoes, Penwood Review, Encore,* and *Sow's Ear.*

www.ingramcontent.com/pod-product-compliance
Lightning Source LLC
LaVergne TN
LVHW050610100826
845148LV00015B/3203

* 9 7 9 8 9 0 1 4 6 8 1 7 3 *